ERIB

Sports and My Body

Dancing

Catherine Veitch

Heinemann Library
Chicago, Illinois

www.heinemannraintree.com
Visit our website to find out
more information about
Heinemann-Raintree books.

To order:

☎ Phone 888-454-2279

💻 Visit www.heinemannraintree.com
to browse our catalog and order online.

© 2009 Raintree
an imprint of Capstone Global Library, LLC
Chicago, Illinois

Customer Service: 888-454-2279

Visit our website at www.heinemannraintree.com

Edited by Siân Smith, Rebecca Rissman, and
   Charlotte Guillain
Designed by Joanna Hinton-Malivoire
Picture research by Ruth Blair
Production by Duncan Gilbert

Originated by Chroma Graphics (Overseas) Pte. Ltd
Printed and bound in China by South China Printing
Company Ltd

13 12 11 10 09
10 9 8 7 6 5 4 3 2 1

Library of Congress Cataloging-in-Publication
Veitch, Catherine.
  Dancing / Catherine Veitch.
    p. cm. -- (Sports and my body)
  Includes bibliographical references and index.
  ISBN 978-1-4329-3501-6 (hb) -- ISBN 978-1-4329-
3502-3 (pb) 1. Dance--Juvenile literature. I. Title.
GV1596.5V45 2008
  792.8--dc22
                                    2009008962

Acknowledgments
The author and publishers are grateful to the following
for permission to reproduce copyright material: Alamy
pp. **7** (© Olivier Asselin), **18** (© Radius Images), **23** (©
Olivier Asselin); Corbis pp. **15**, **4**, **21**, **23** (Fancy/Veer),
6, **23** (The Irish Image Collection), **8** (Tim Pannell), **9**
(Tom Stewart), **12** (Martin Harvey), **16** (Anna Peisl/zefa),
17 (Gideon Mendel), **20** (David Ashley); Getty Images
pp. **5** (Chris Jackson), **10** (Jim Esposito/Taxi), **11** (David
Handley/DK), **13** (Paul Chesley), **19** (Frank Siteman), **23**
(Paul Chesley); Photolibrary pp. **14**, **23** (Tetra Images);
Shutterstock pp. **22 top left**, **22 top right**, **22
bottom left**, **22 bottom right** (MalibuBooks).

Cover photograph of a boy dancing reproduced with
permission of Punchstock/Photodisc. Back cover images
reproduced with permission of the following: 1. dancer
stretching leg (Photolibrary/© Tetra Images); a pair of
pumps (Shutterstock).

Every effort has been made to contact copyright holders
of material reproduced in this book. Any omissions will
be rectified in subsequent printings if notice is given to
the publishers.

Disclaimer
All the Internet addresses (URLs) given in this book were
valid at the time of going to press. However, due to the
dynamic nature of the Internet, some addresses may
have changed, or sites may have changed or ceased to
exist since publication. While the author and publishers
regret any inconvenience this may cause readers, no
responsibility for any such changes can be accepted by
either the author or the publishers.

Contents

Some words are shown in bold, **like this**. You can find them in the glossary on page 23.

What Is Dancing?

When we move to music we are dancing. Dancing is a type of exercise.

We can use dancing to show how we are feeling. We can show if we are feeling happy, sad, scared, or angry.

What Types of Dance Are There?

There are different types of dance around the world. **Irish dancing** comes from Ireland.

People may wear special clothes and shoes for different types of dance.

How Do I Learn to Dance?

You can learn to dance anywhere.
You can learn in your home or outside.
All you need is some music or a **beat**.

You can learn special types of dance at a dance class. You need an adult to teach you.

How Do I Use My Legs and Feet?

You can use your legs and feet when you jump. You can also use your legs when you turn.

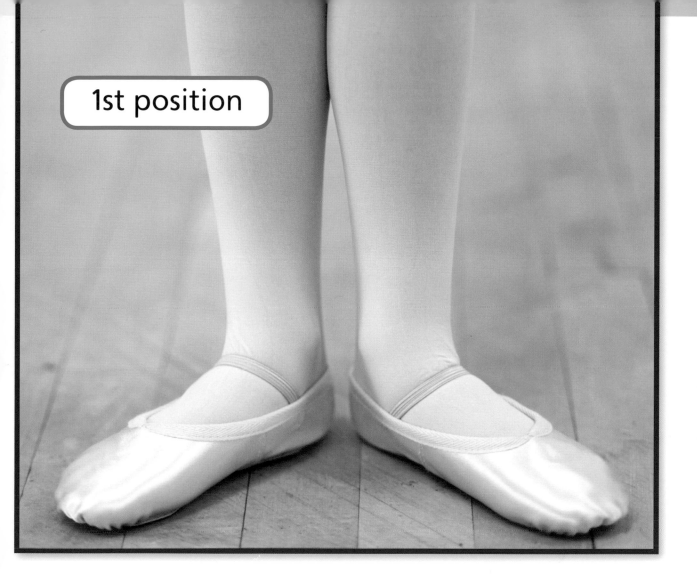

1st position

Where you place your feet is important in dance. In ballet you stand in different **positions**.

How Do I Use My Arms?

You can stretch out your arms to help you **balance**. You can hold your arms in different **positions**.

You can use your arms to show how you feel. You can move your arms slowly or you can move your arms quickly.

What Happens to My Body When I Dance?

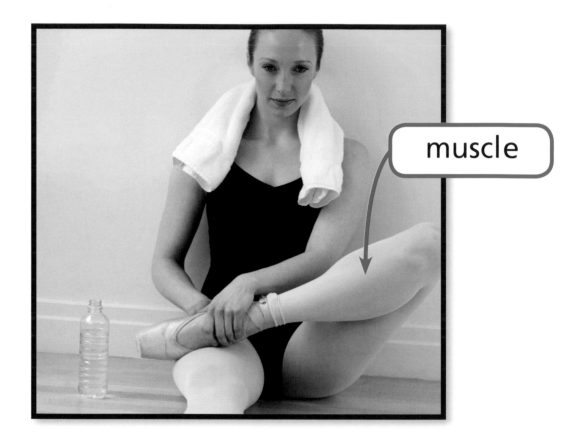

muscle

When you dance your heart will beat faster. Your **muscles** may ache and feel tired.

When you dance you may feel hot and sweaty. You will also feel thirsty.

How Does It Feel to Dance?

You might feel happy when you dance. You may also make good friends as you dance together.

It is fun to watch dance. People like to watch dance together.

Have you ever watched dancers?

How Do I Stay Safe Dancing?

muscle

You should always warm up before you dance. Gentle jumping and swinging your arms and legs will warm up your **muscles**.

It is important to listen to your dance teacher. Your teacher will show you how to move safely.

Does Dancing Make Me Healthy?

Dancing is good exercise and will help you to keep fit. You should also eat healthy food and drink plenty of water.

To stay healthy you need to get plenty of rest, too. Then you can have fun in many different ways.

Dancing Shoes

ballet shoes

running shoes

sneakers

tap shoes

Glossary

 **balance** keep yourself or an object steady so that it does not fall

 **beat** in music this is a regular sound, sometimes made by a drum. Listening to the beat can help you to keep in time with the music.

 **Irish dancing** traditional type of dance that began in Ireland

 **muscle** part of your body that helps you to move. Exercise can make muscles bigger and stronger.

 **position** place where something is. We put our arms in different positions when we move them around and use them to make different shapes.

Index

Find Out More

www.activitytv.com/dance-for-kids
This Website features videos that will teach you all kinds of dance moves.

www.nycballet.com/families/families.html
On this Website for the New York City Ballet, you will find a glossary of ballet terms, crossword puzzles, and more about ballet.